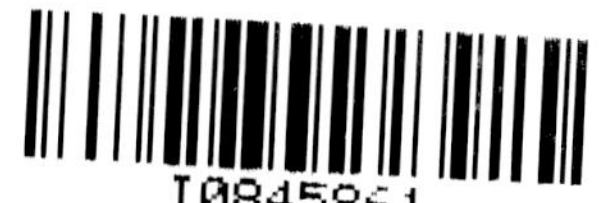
I0845861

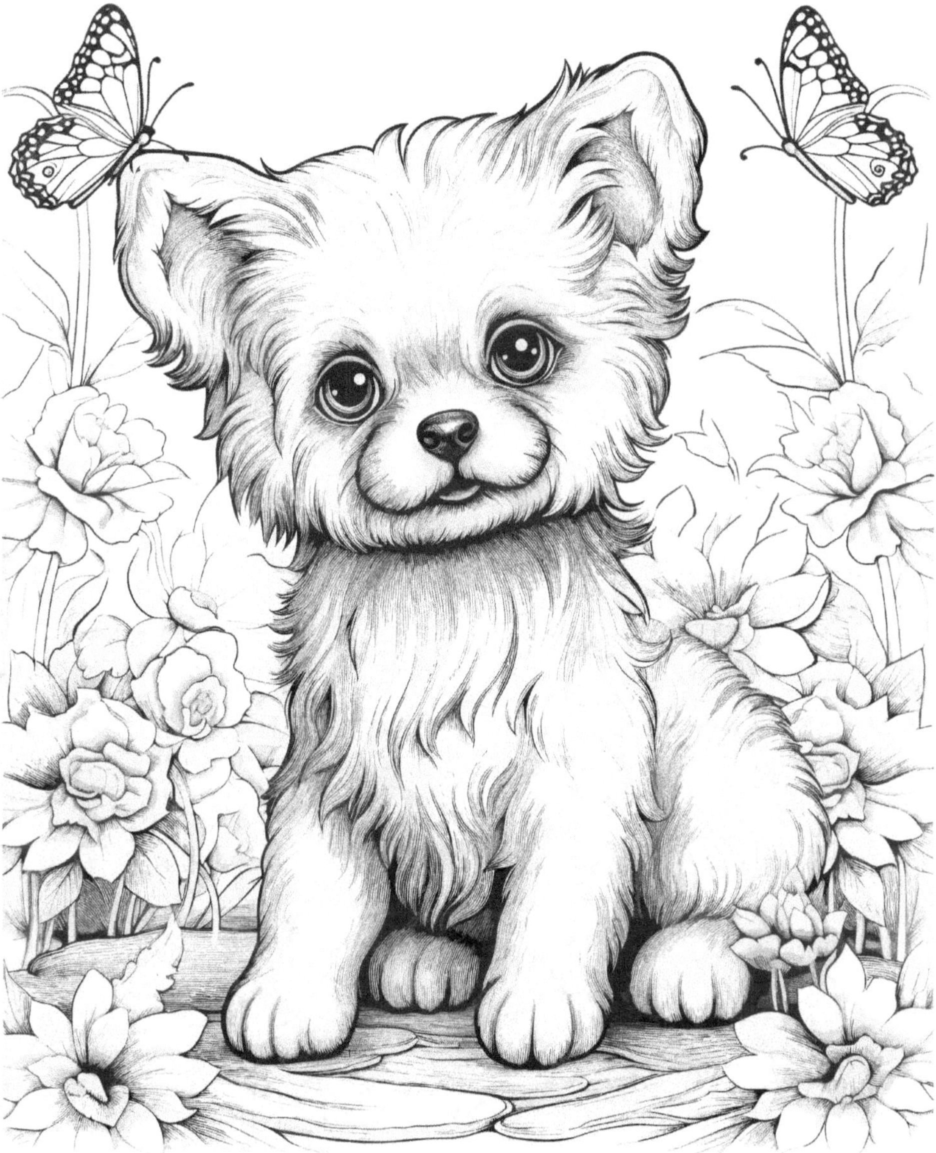

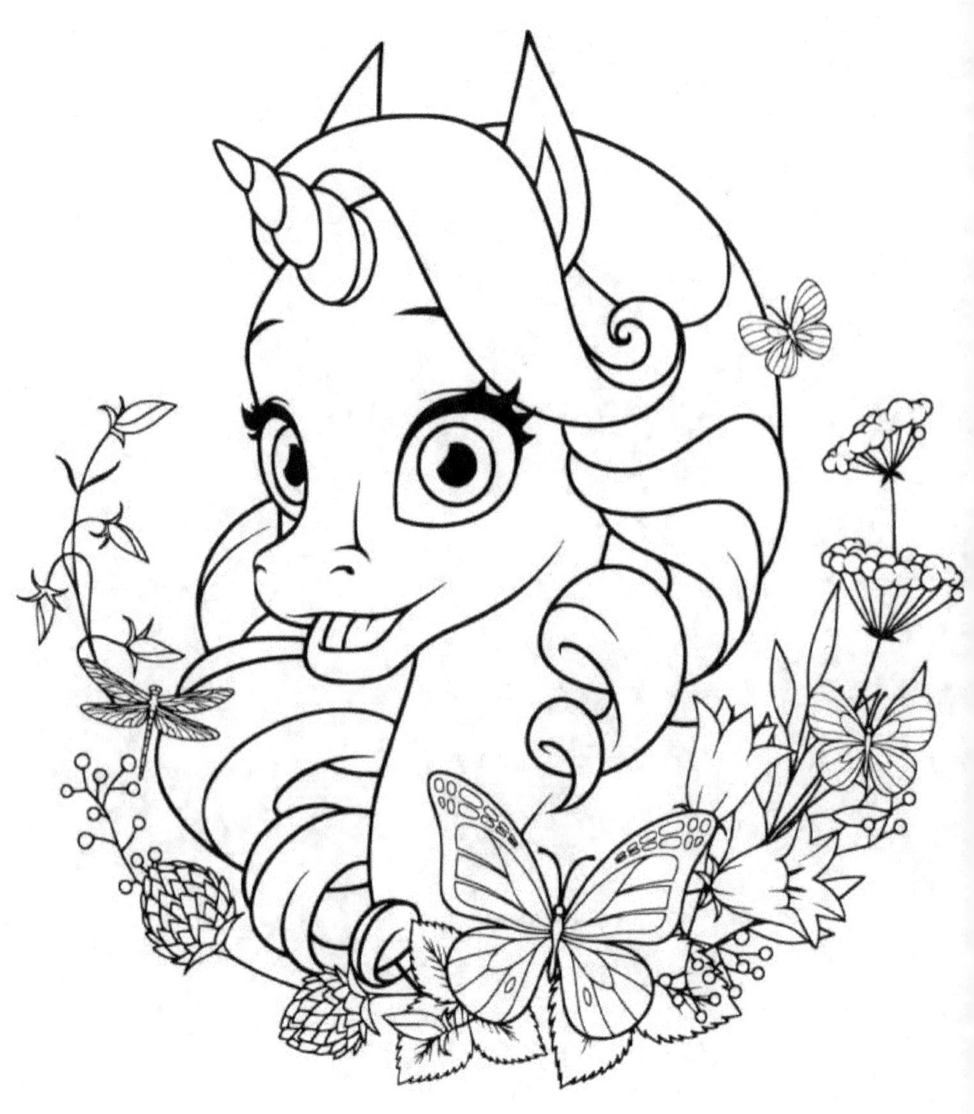

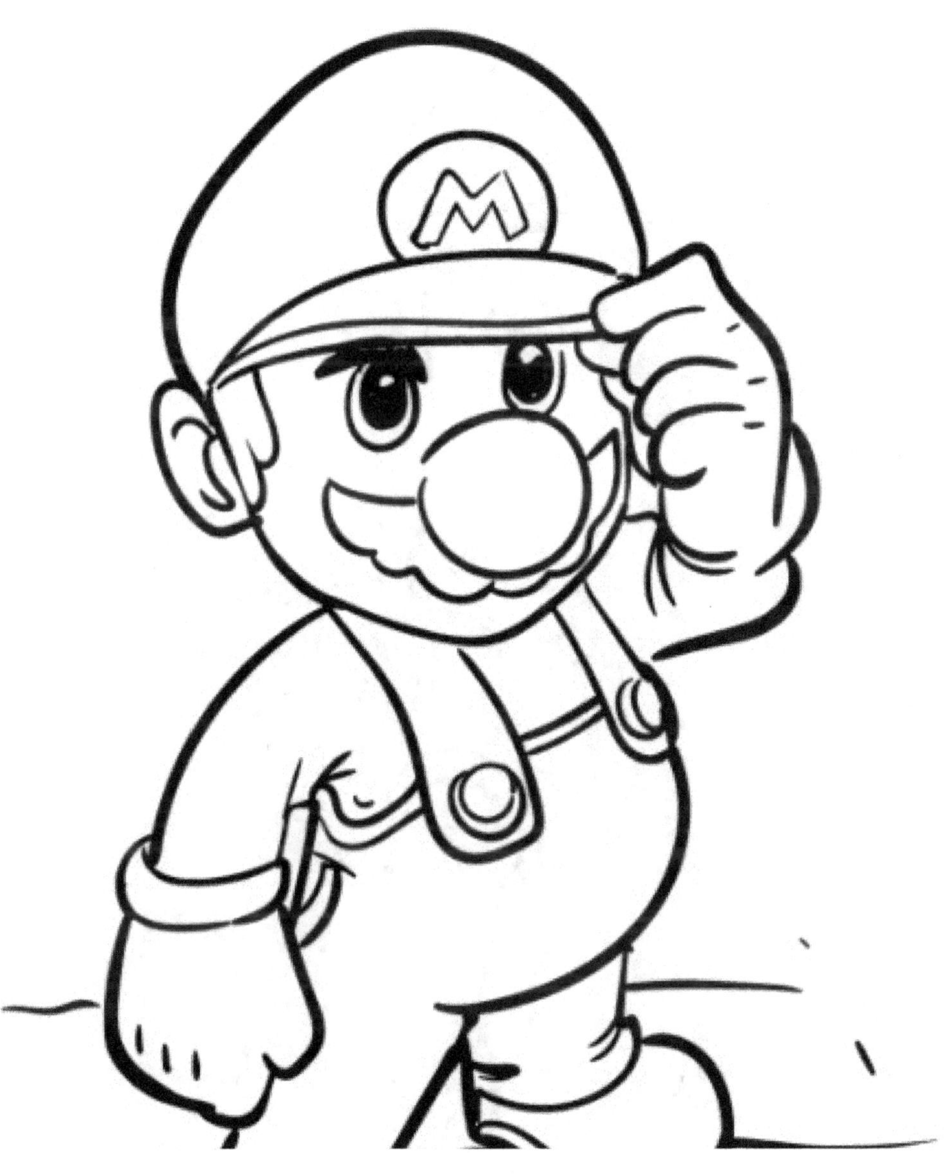

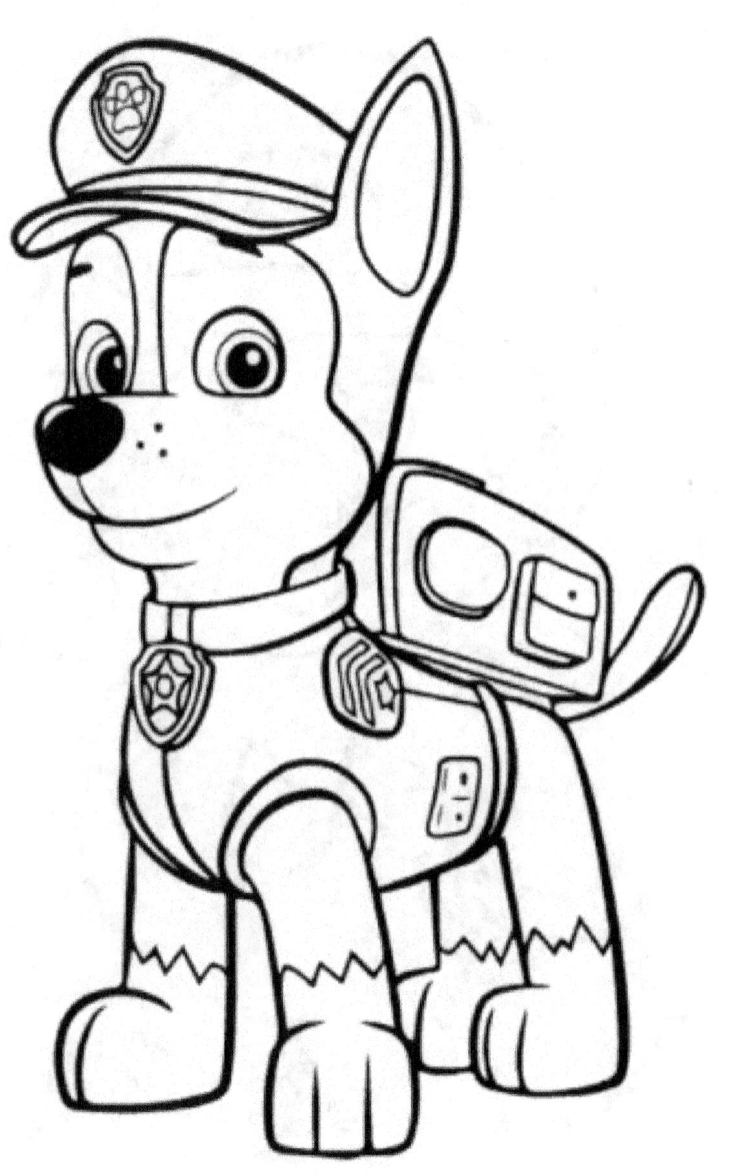

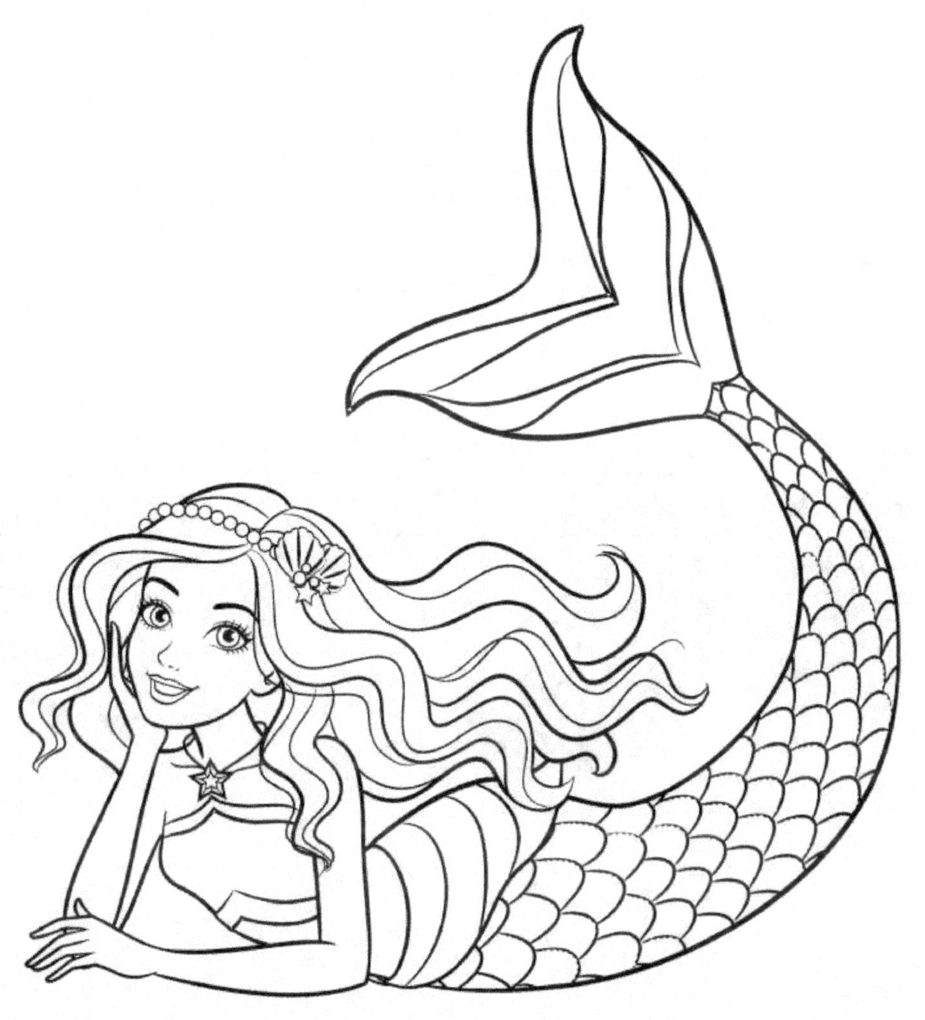

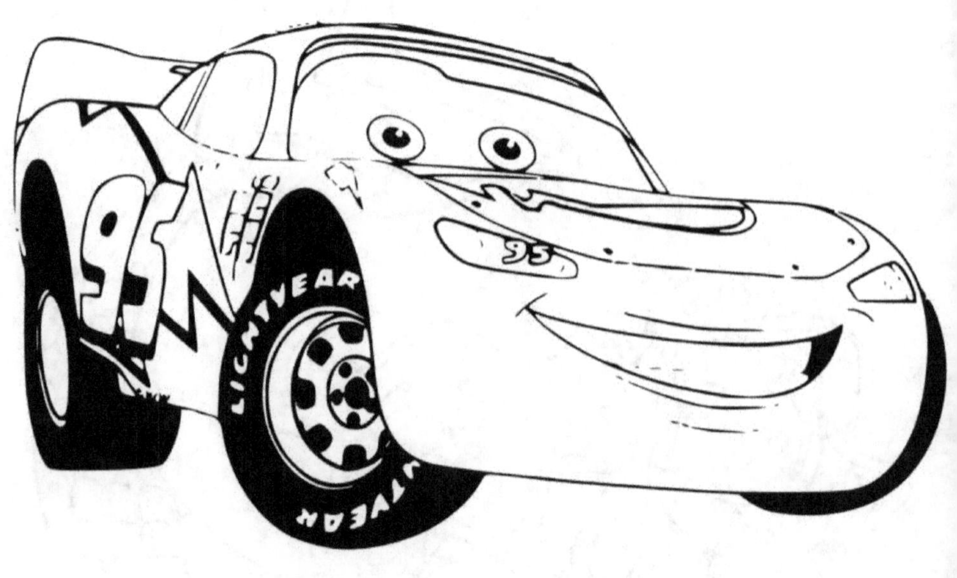
95
LIGHTYEAR
95

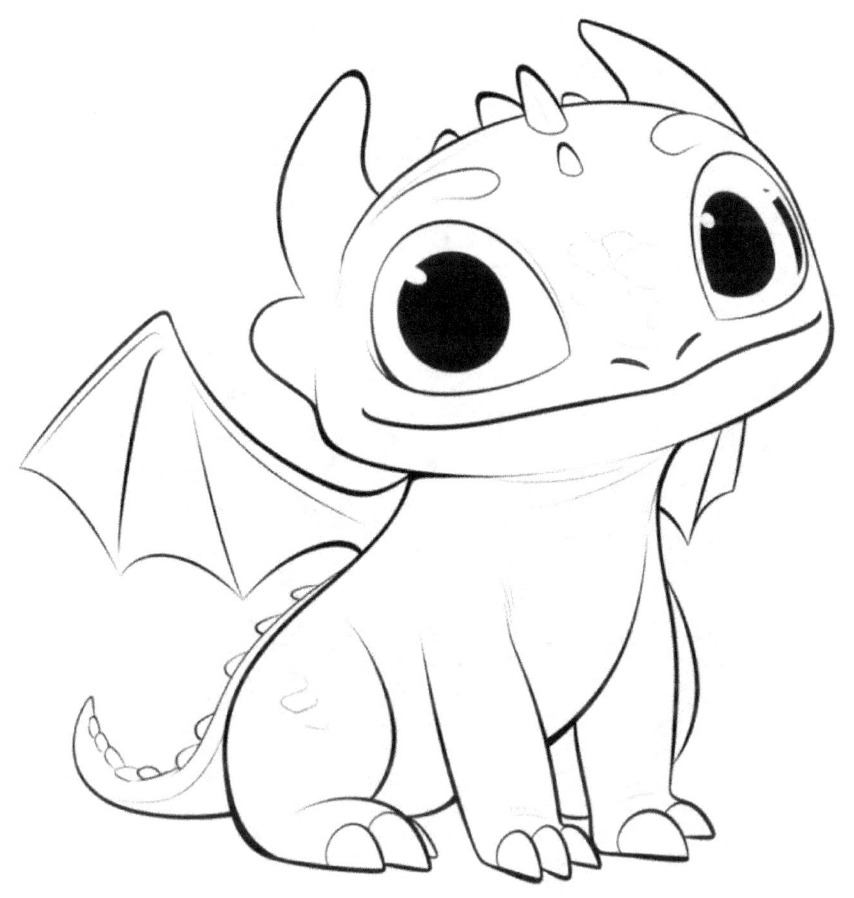

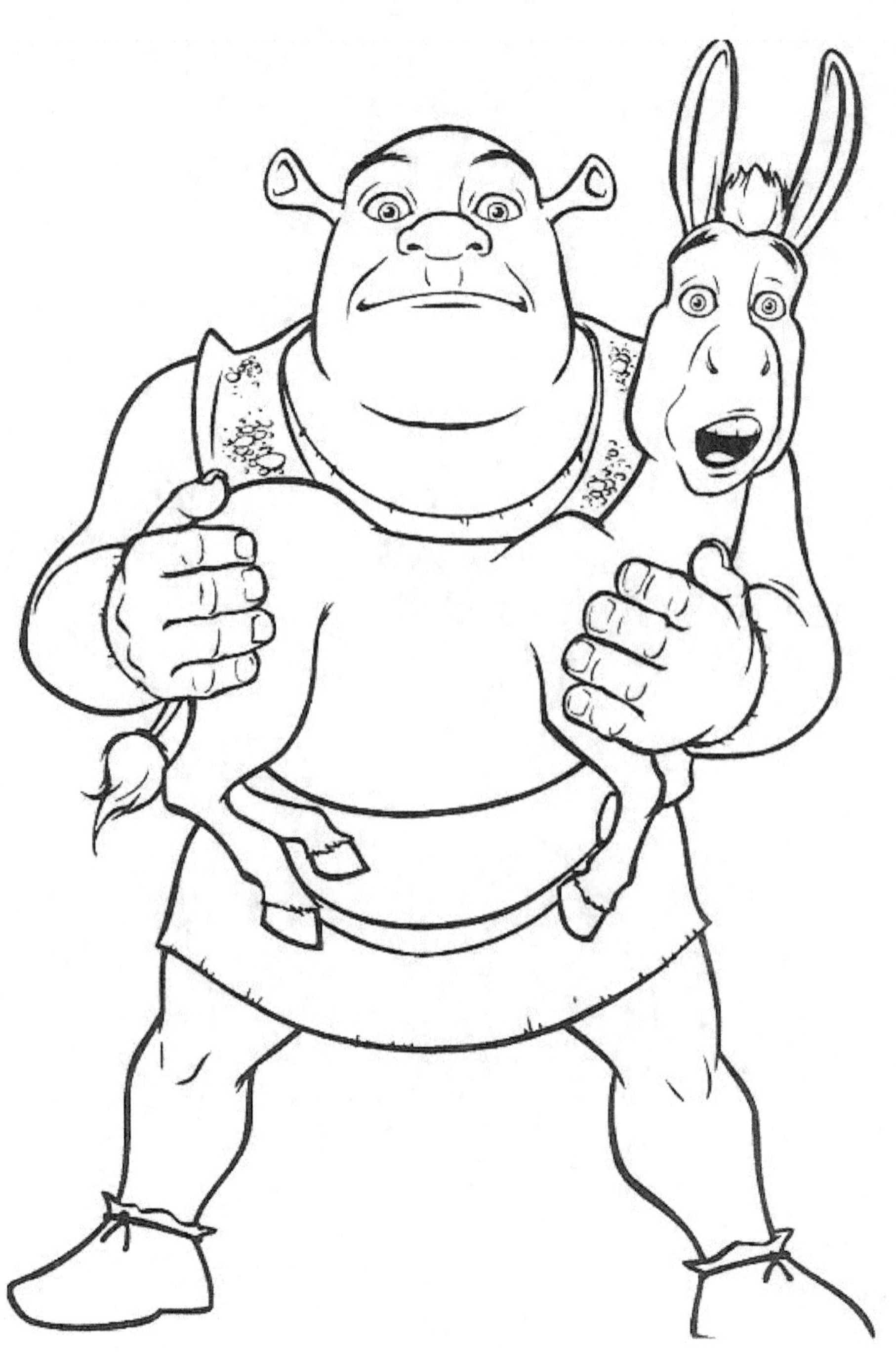

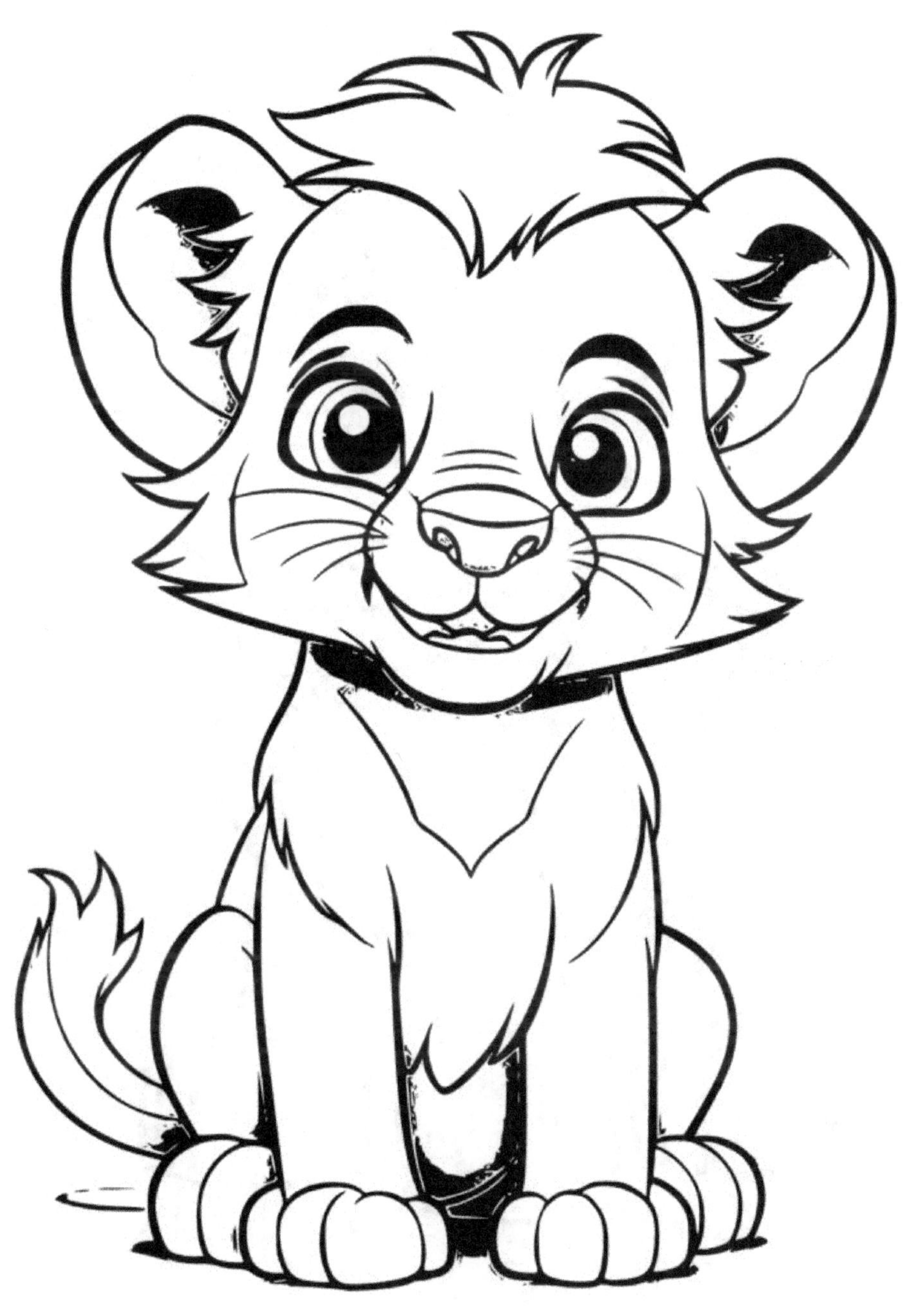

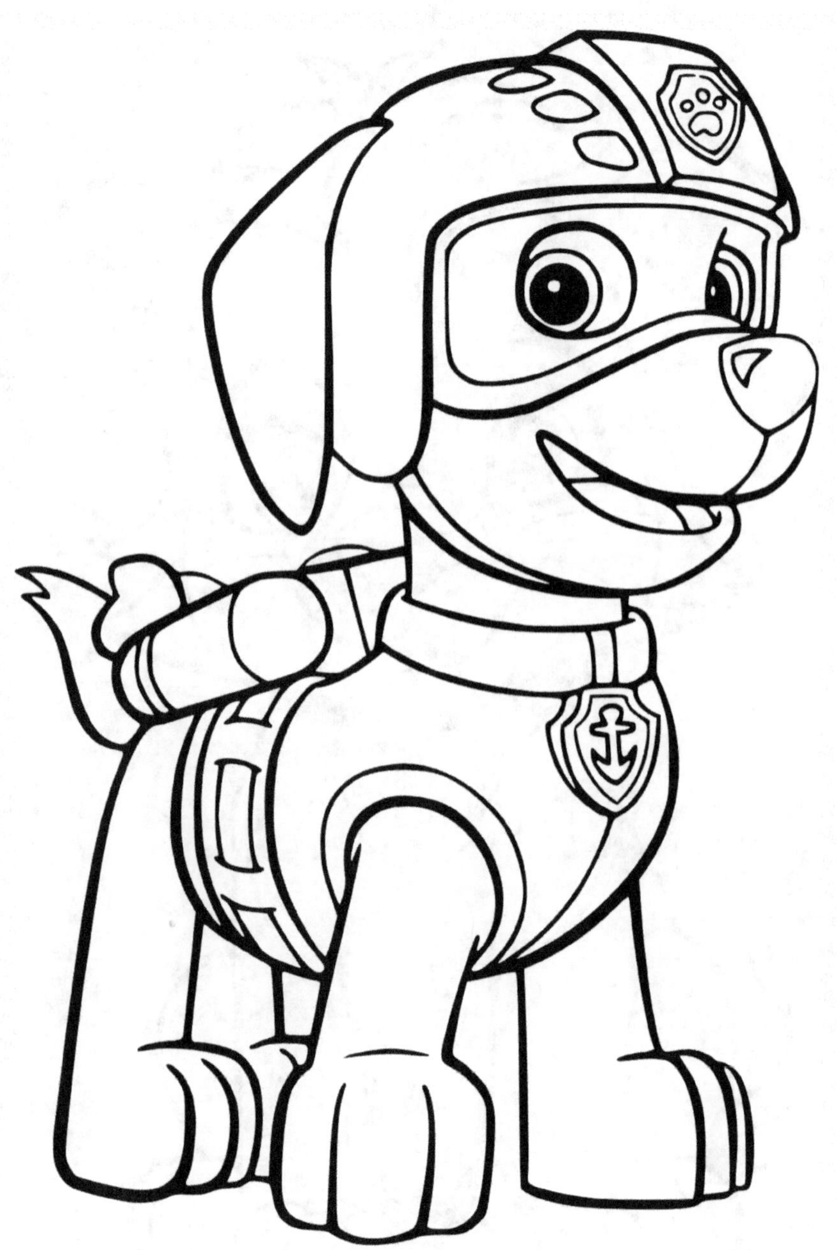

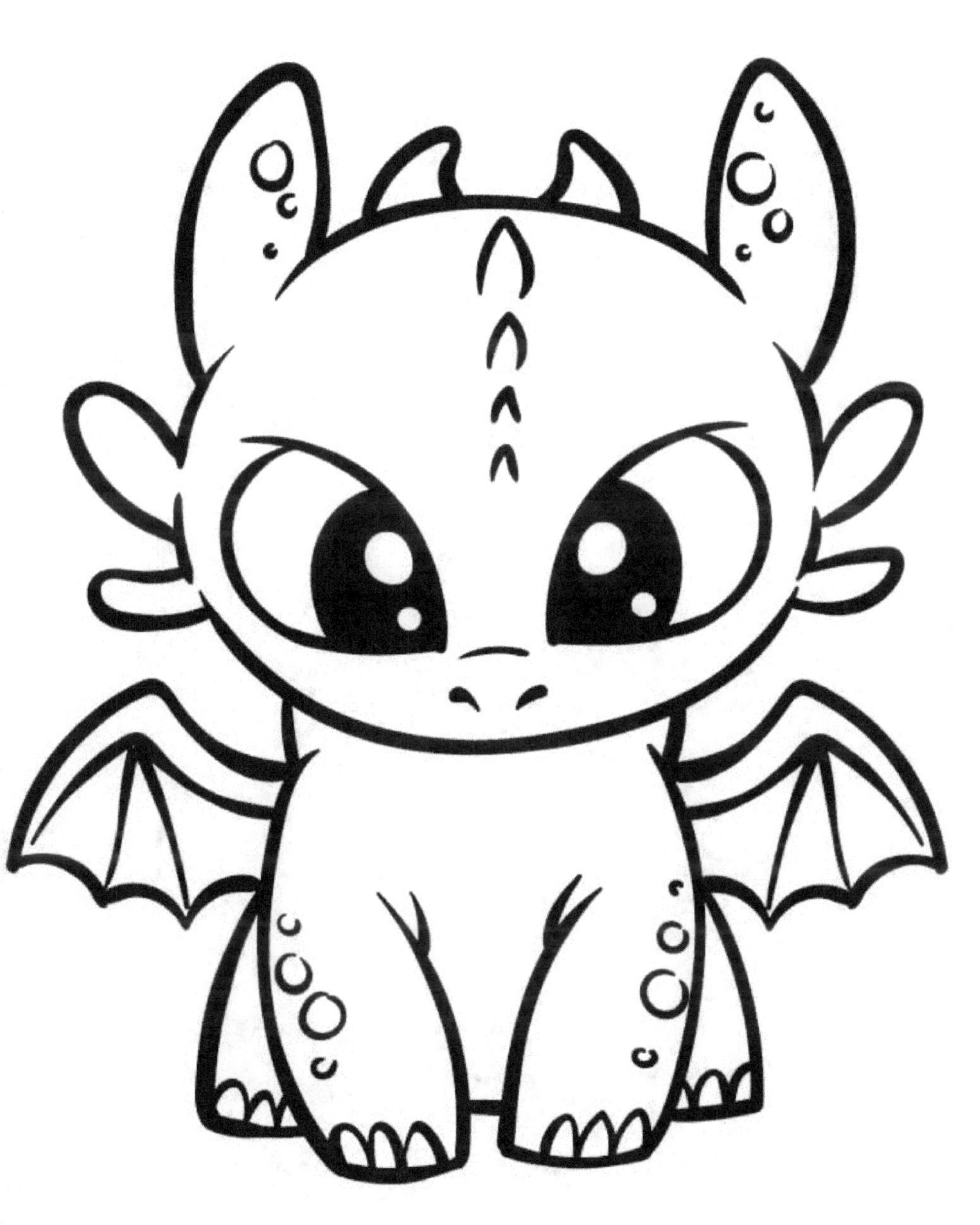

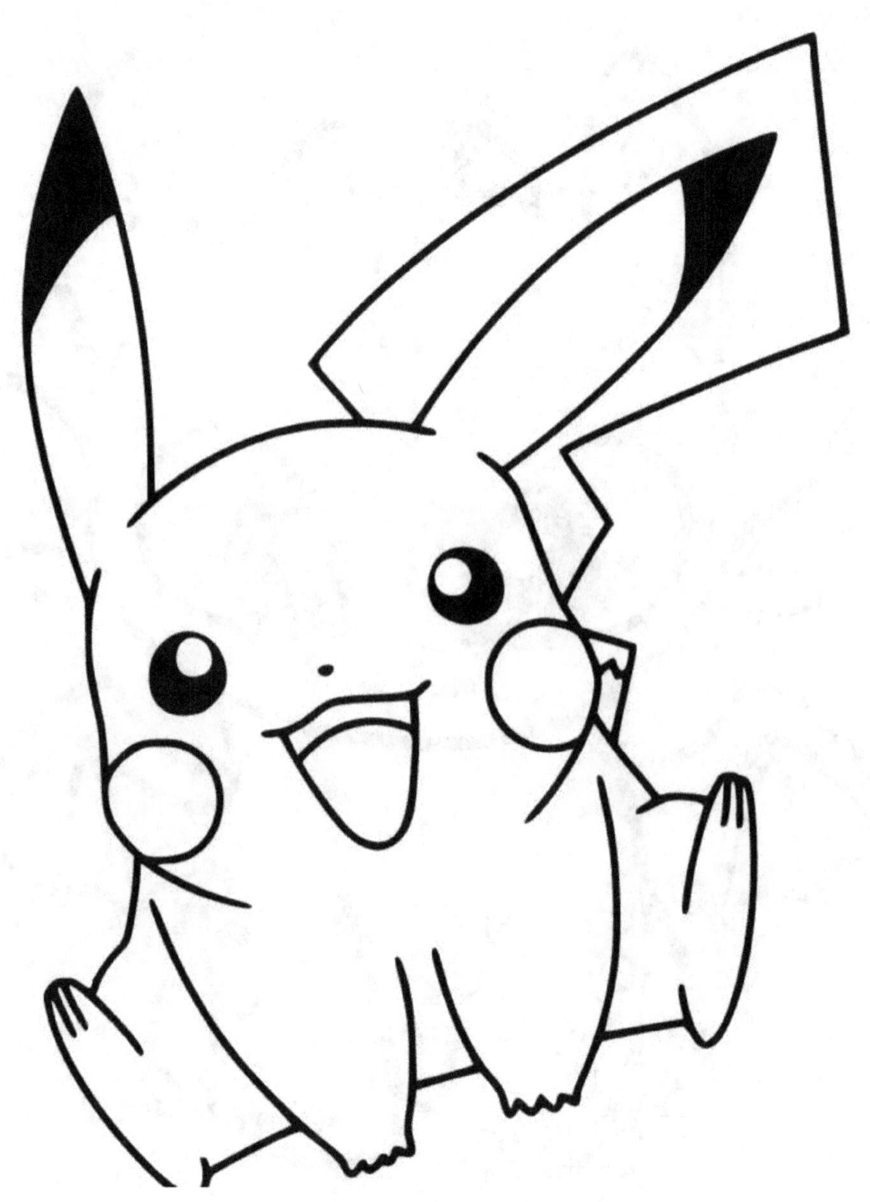

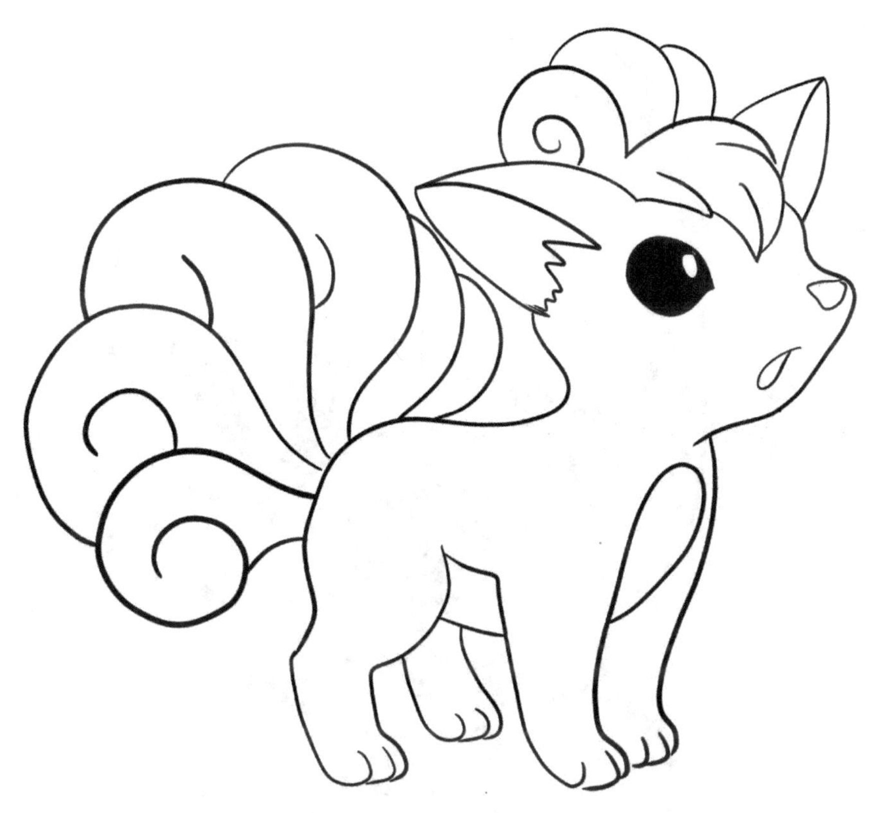

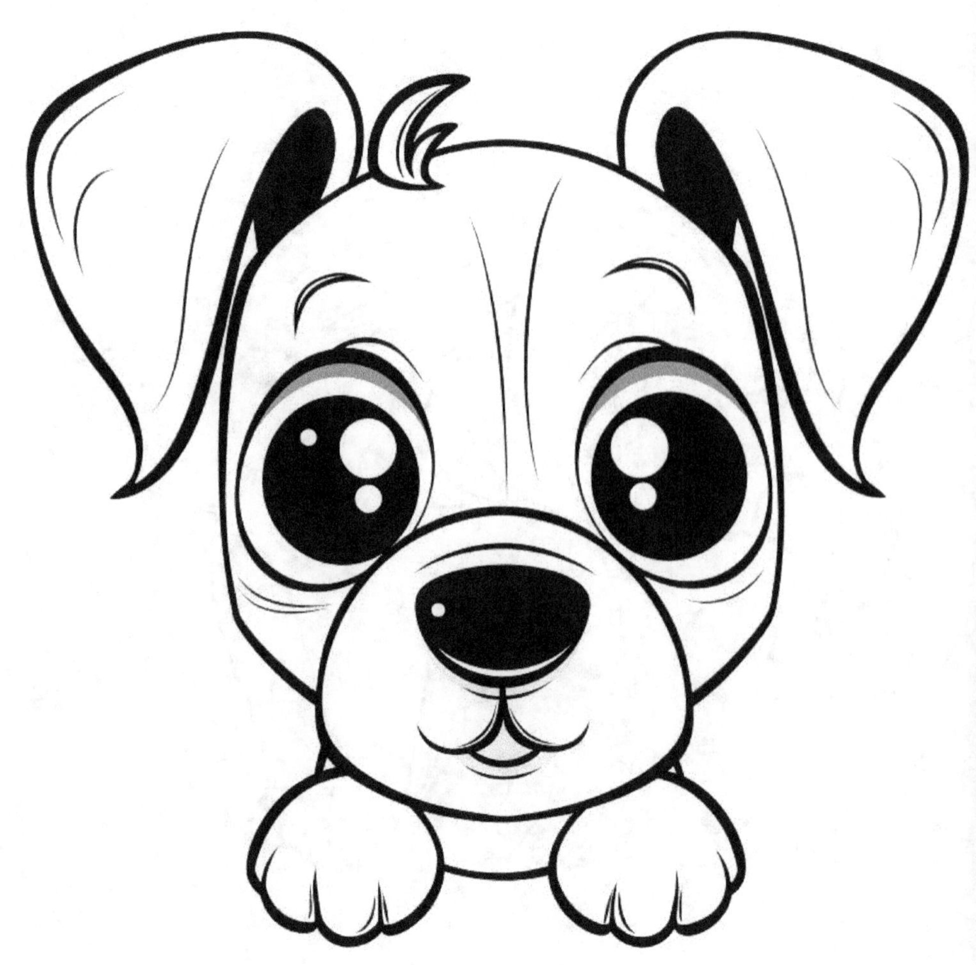

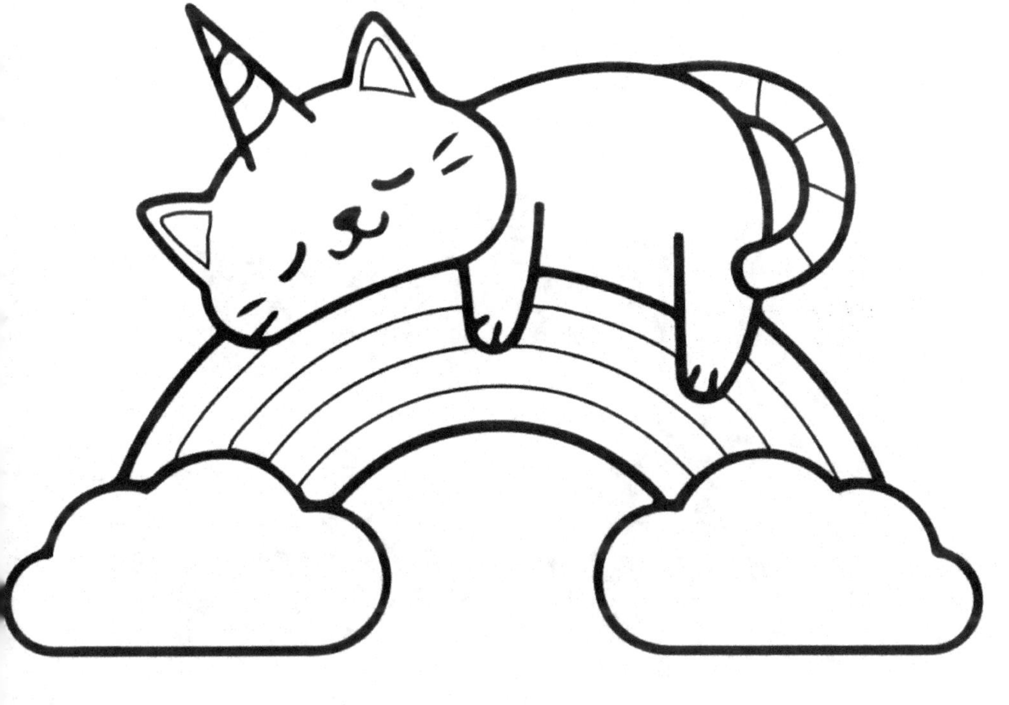

Time For More Practical Exercises

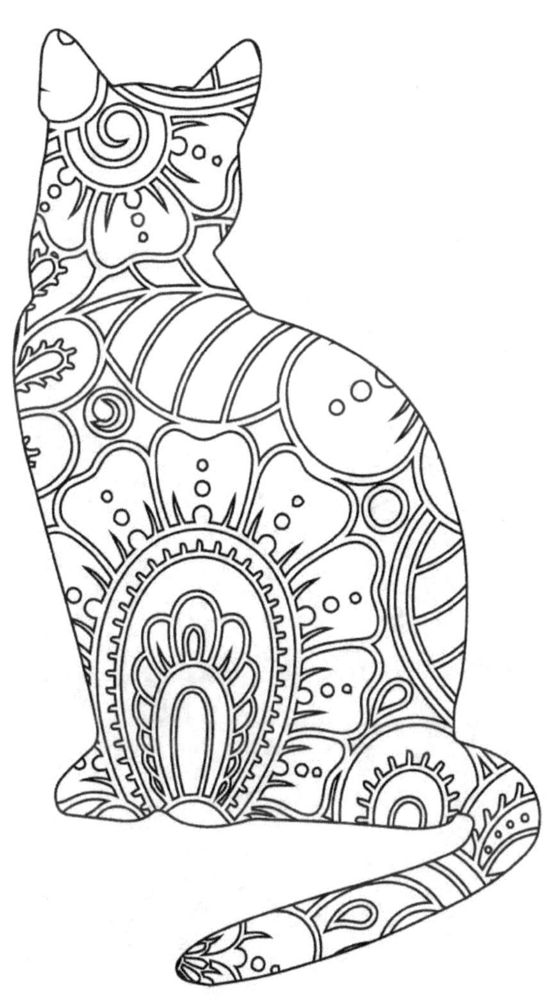

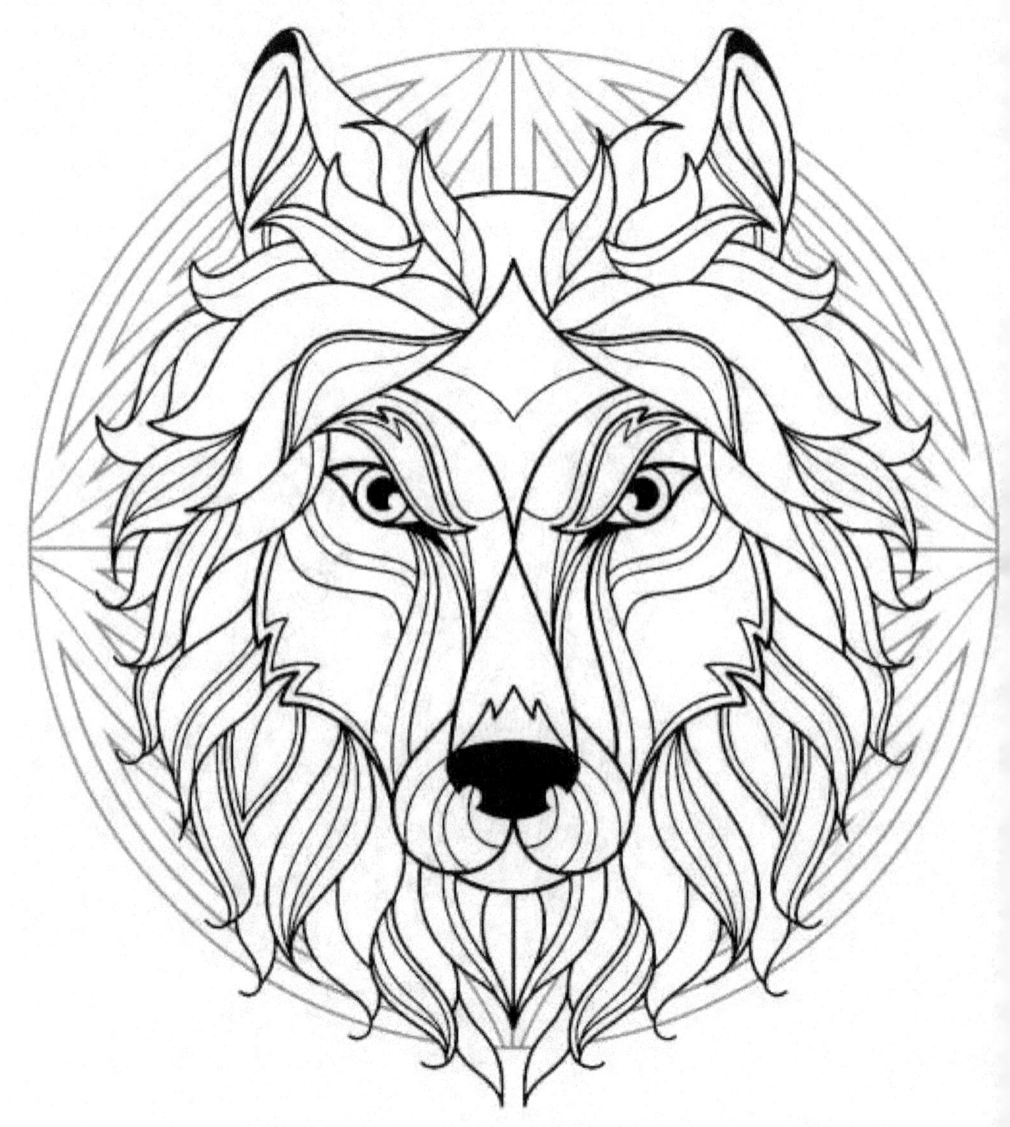

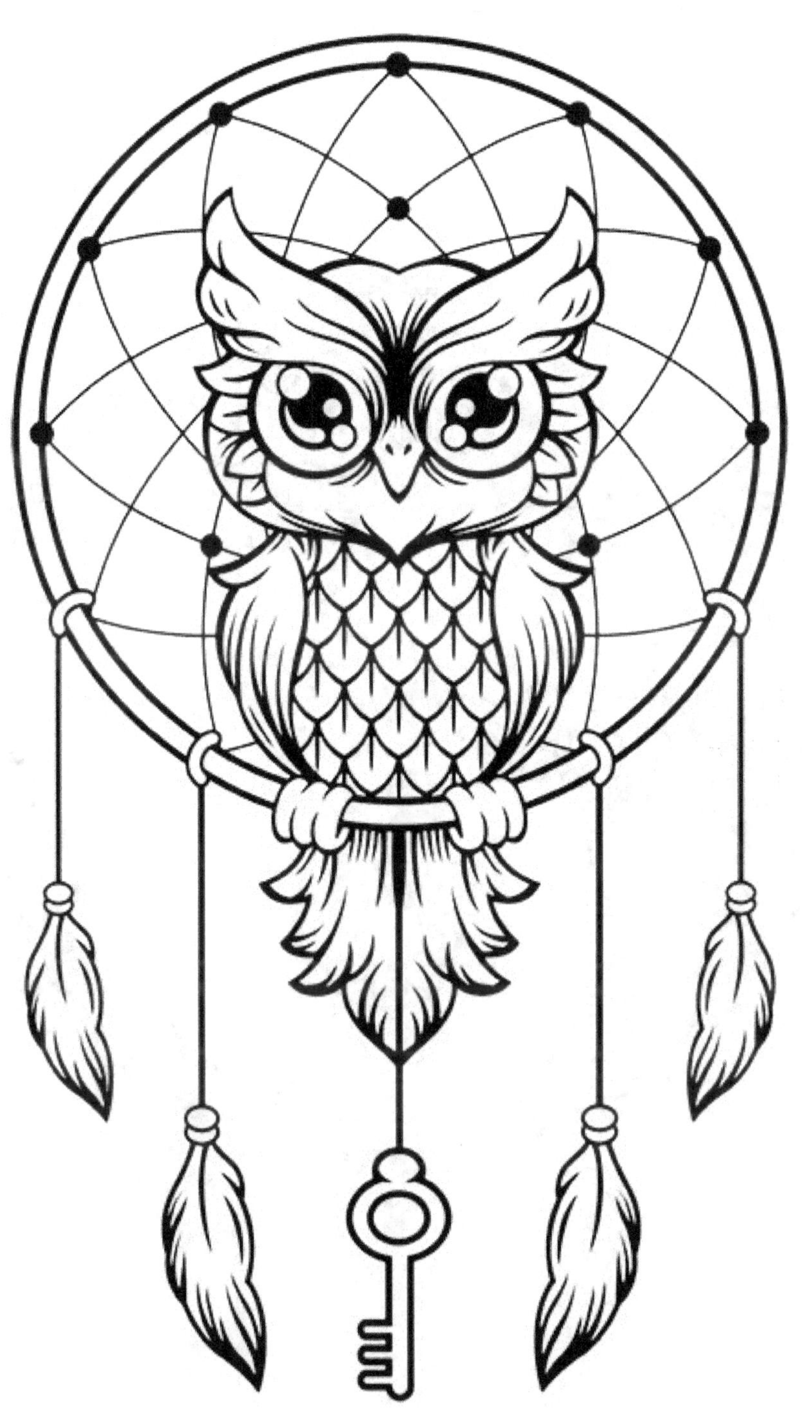

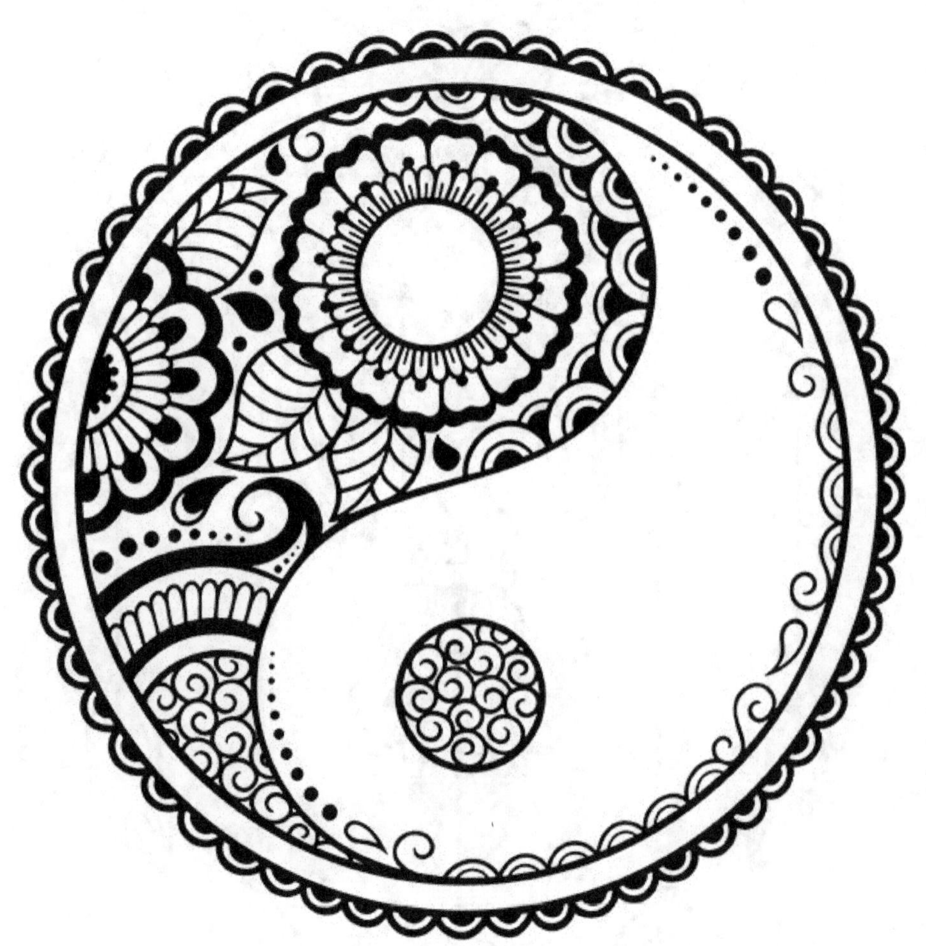

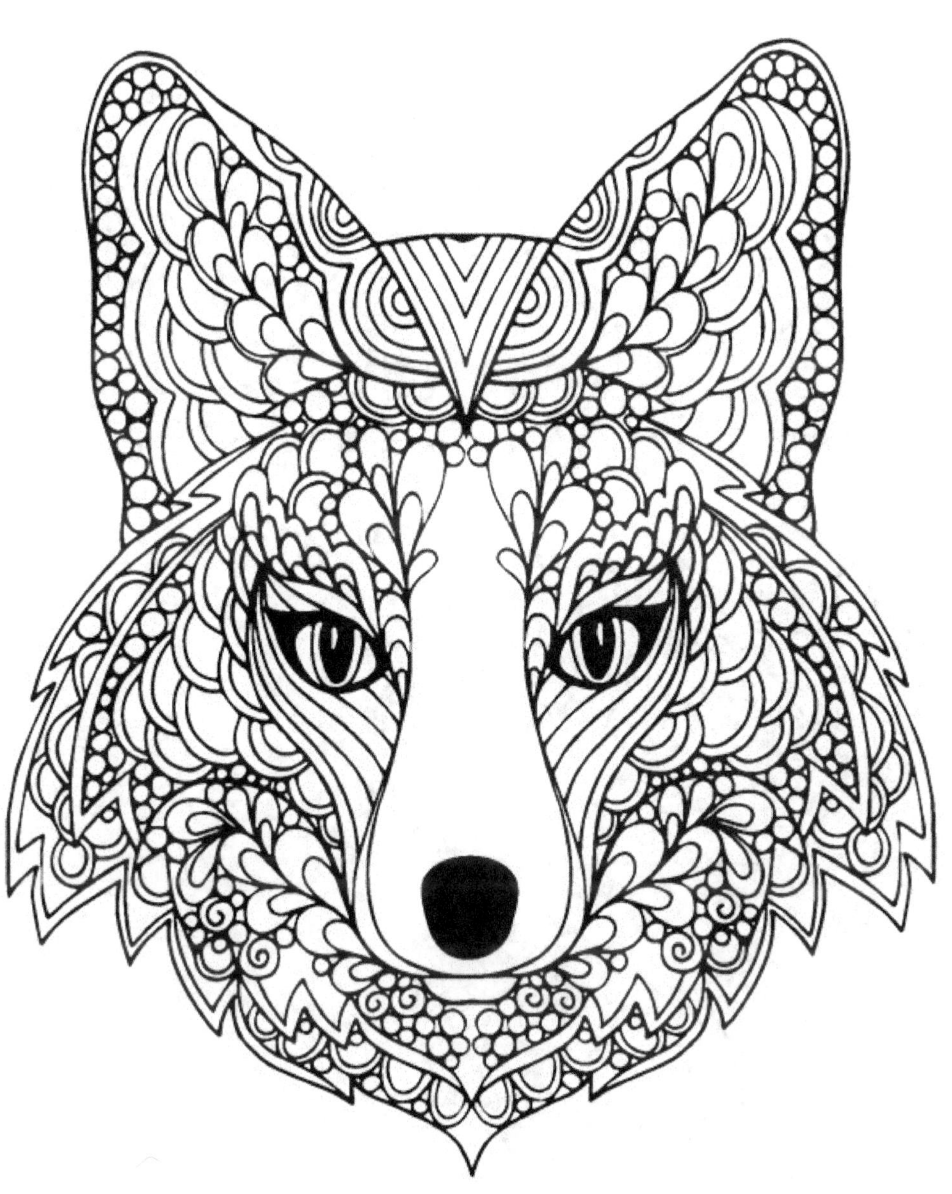

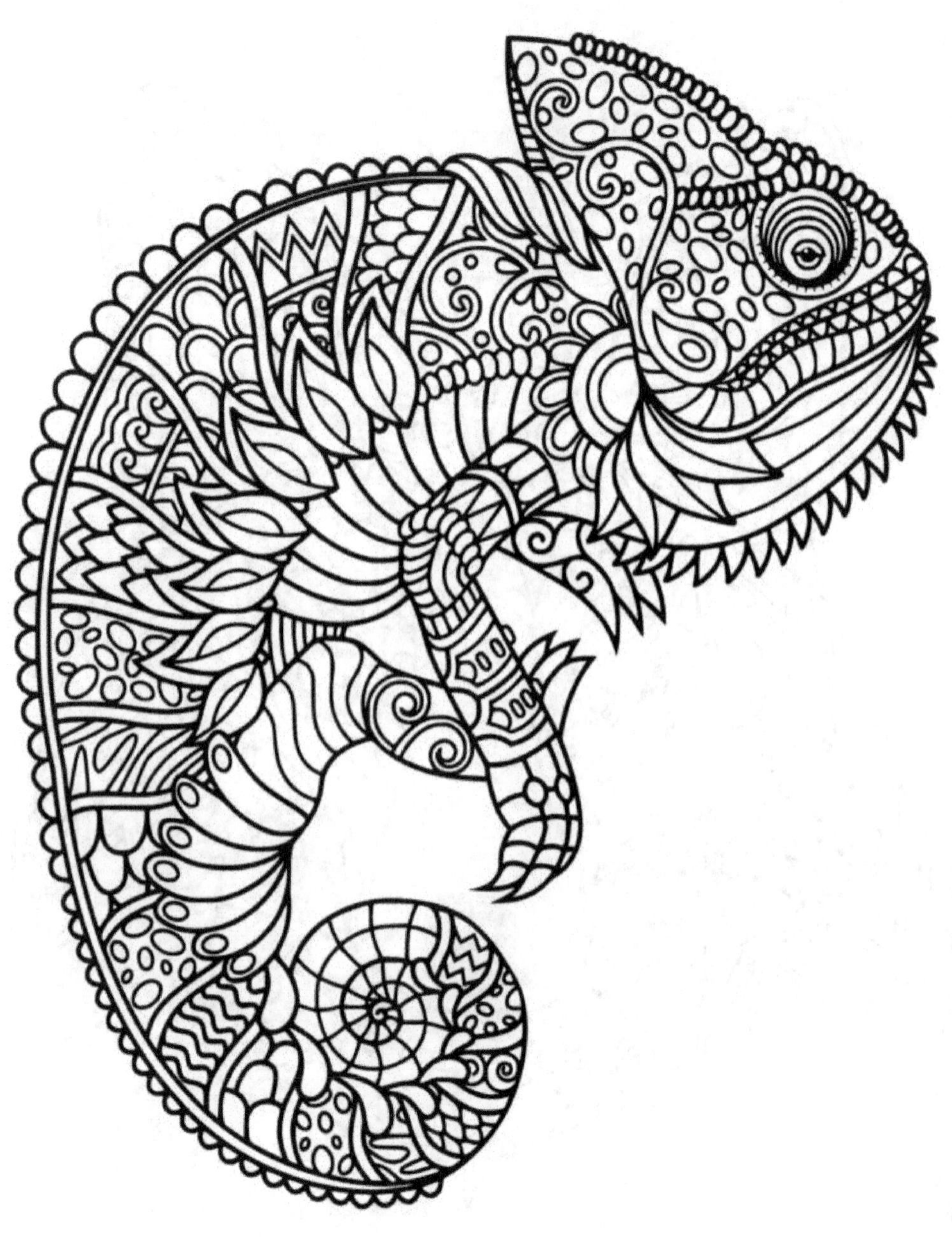

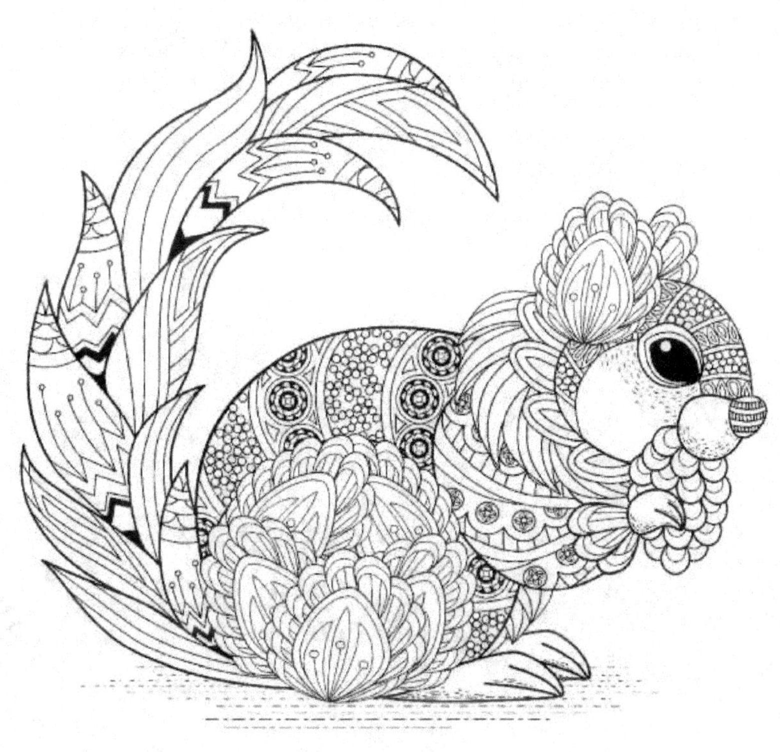

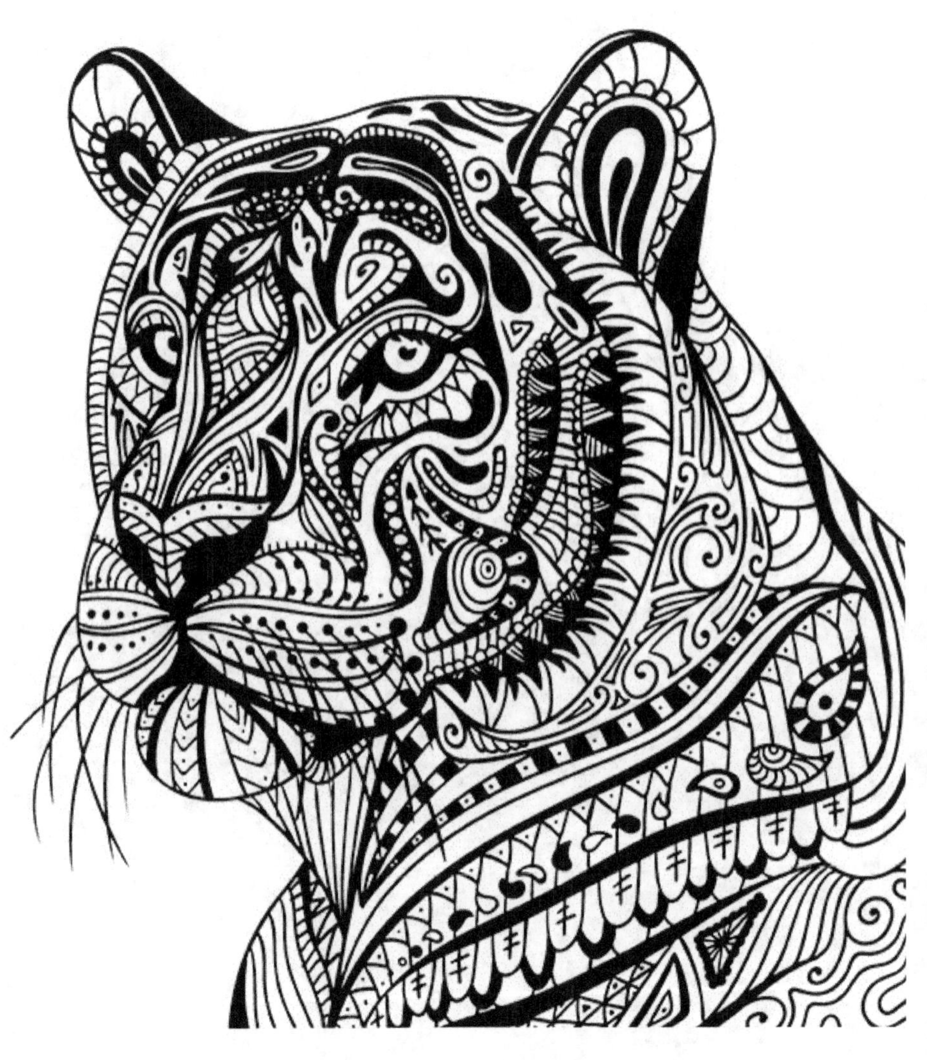

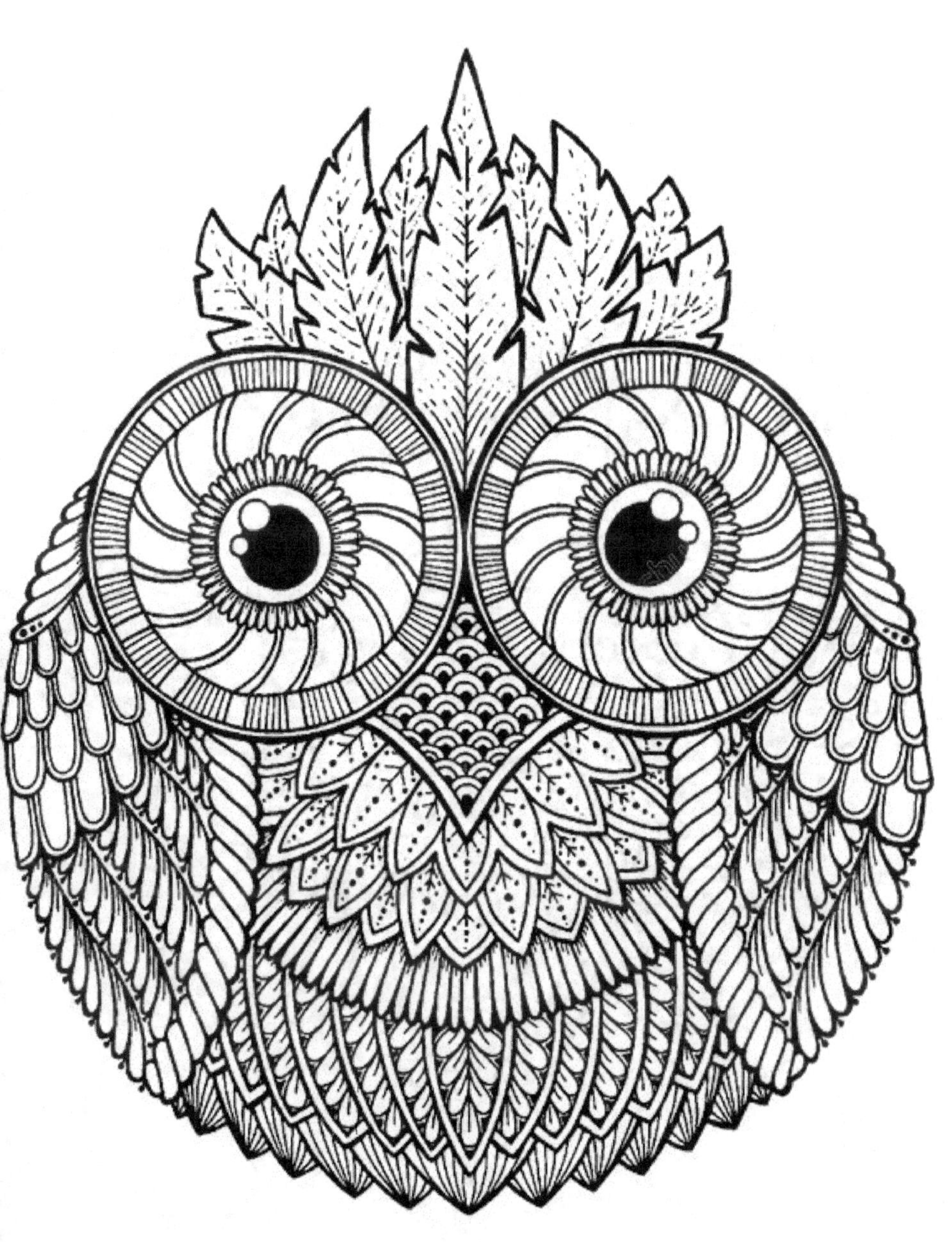

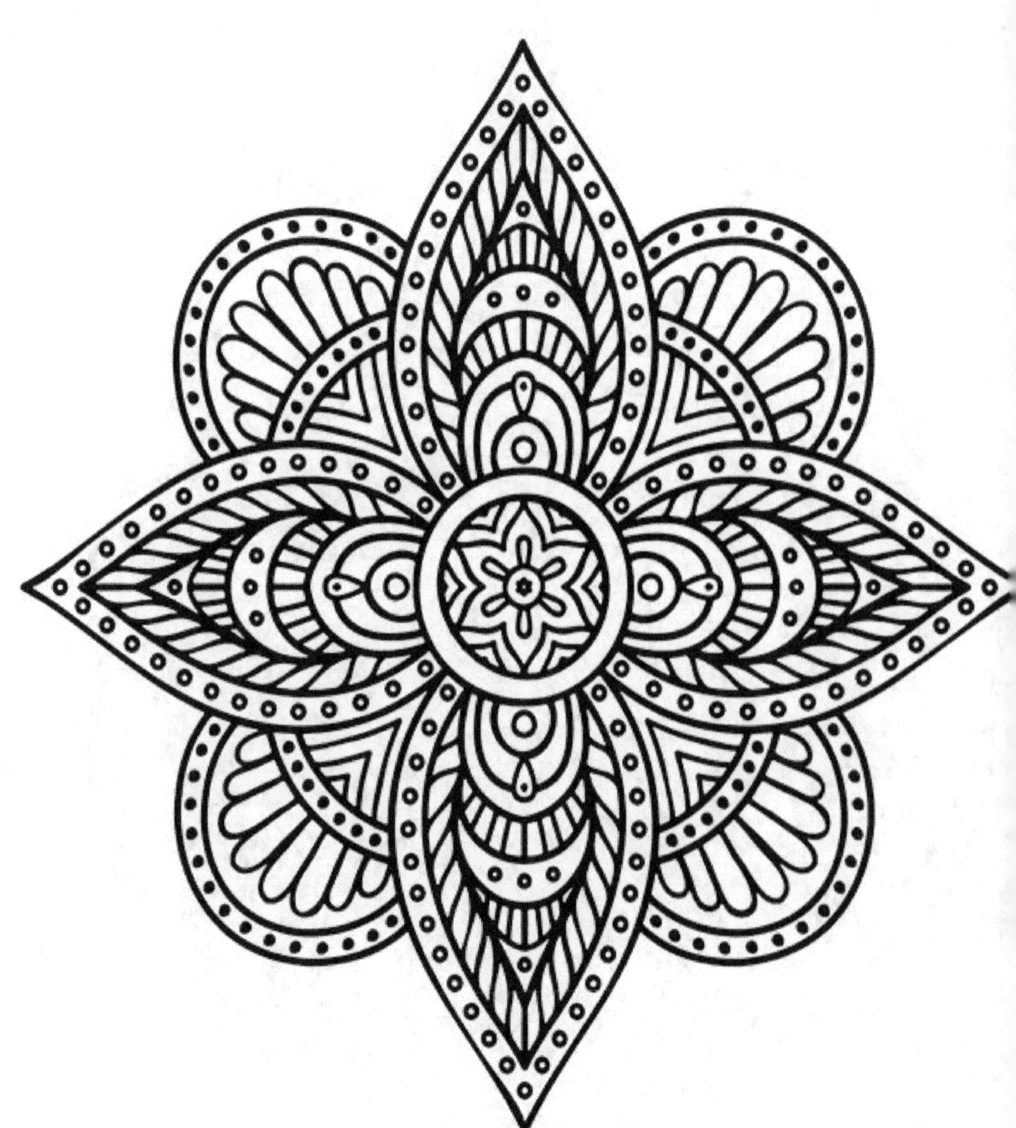

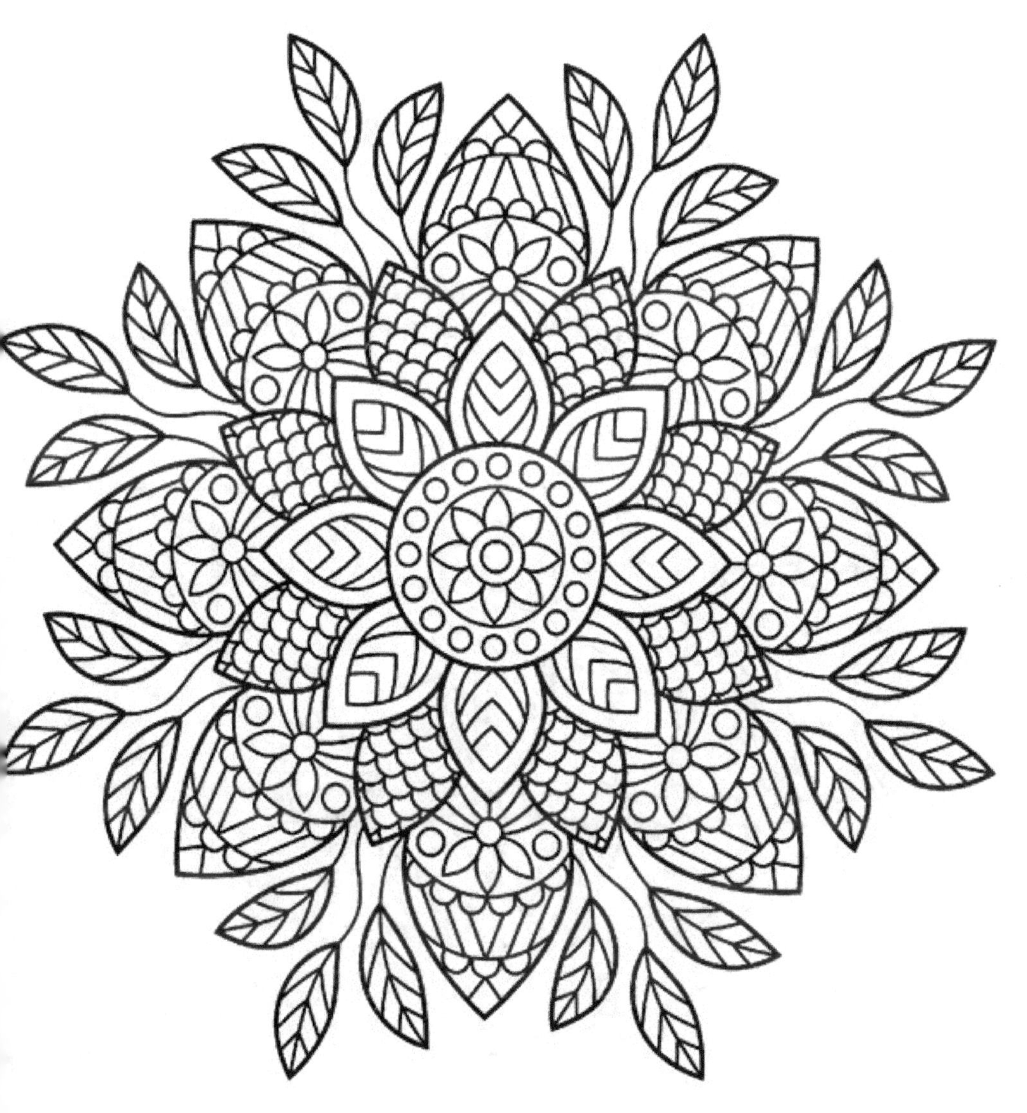

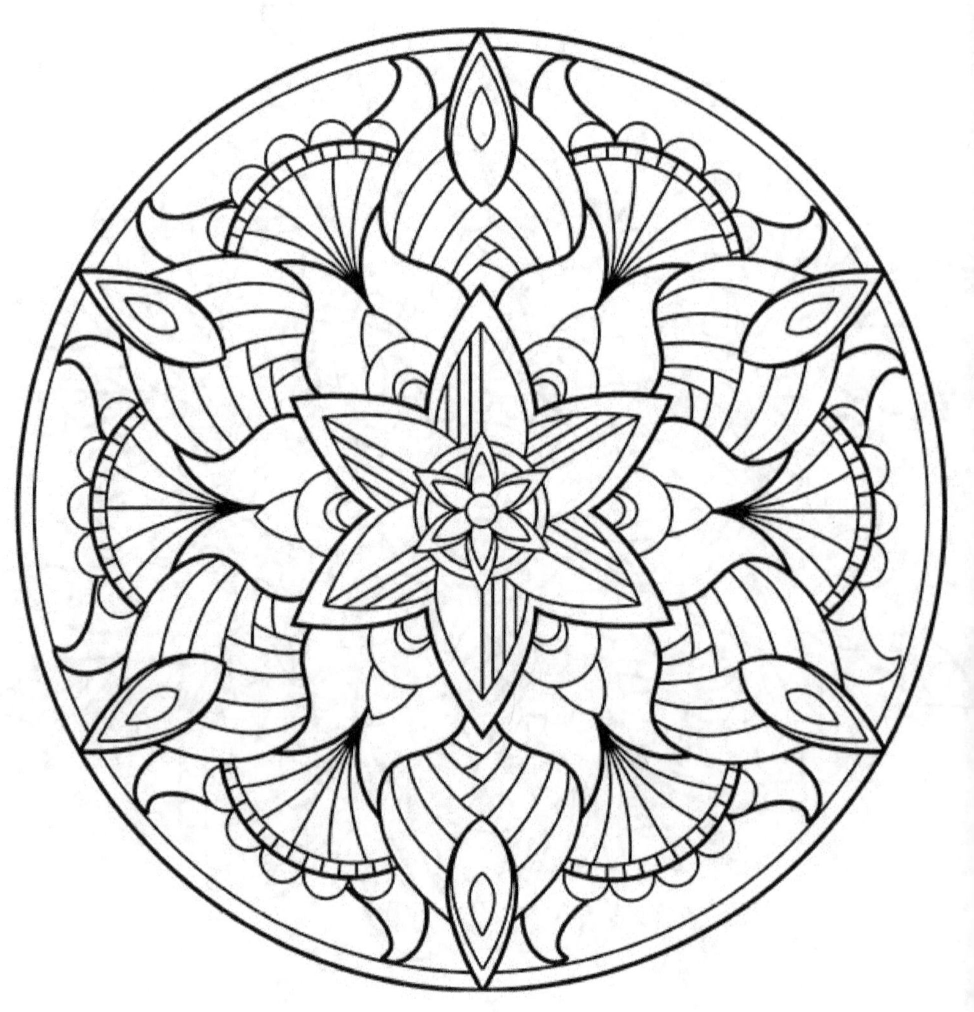

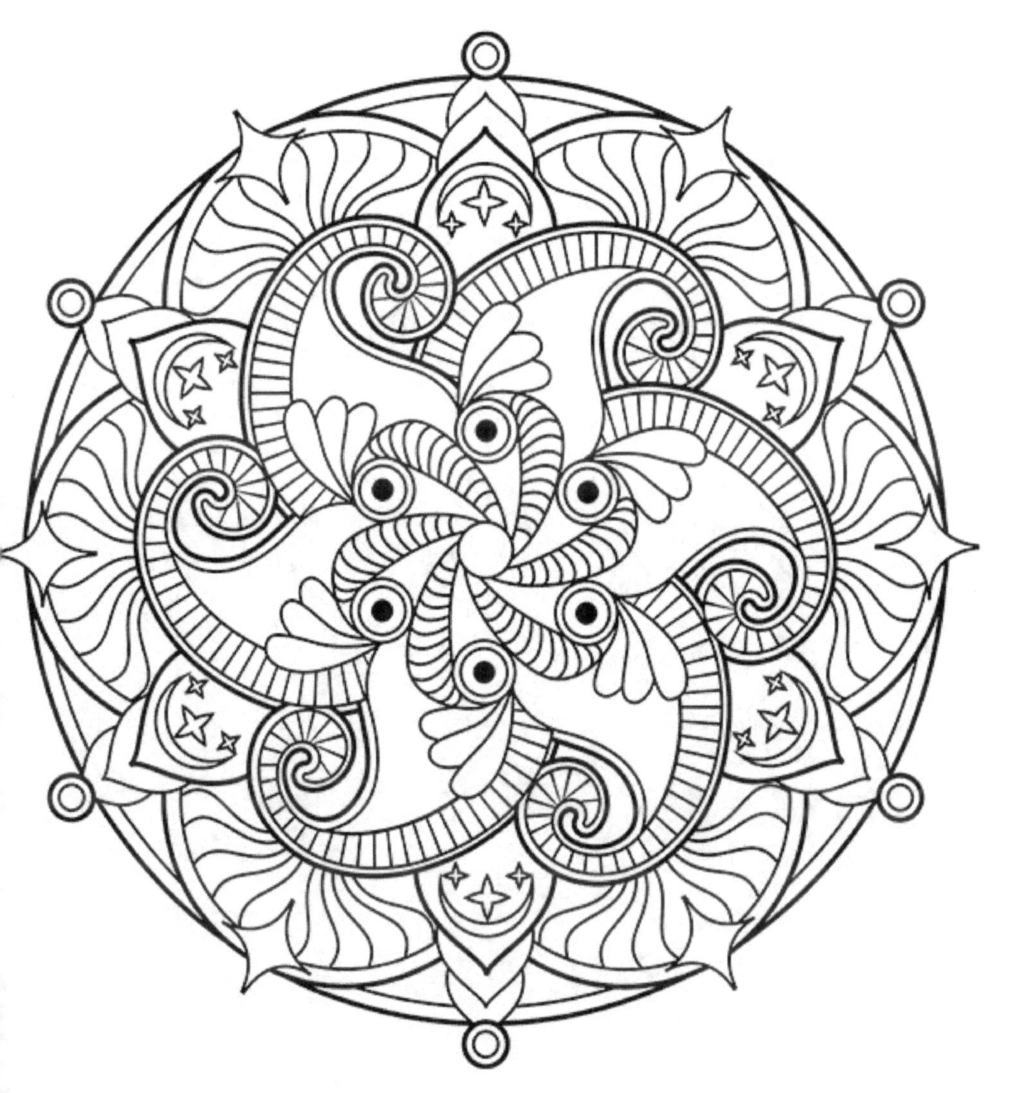

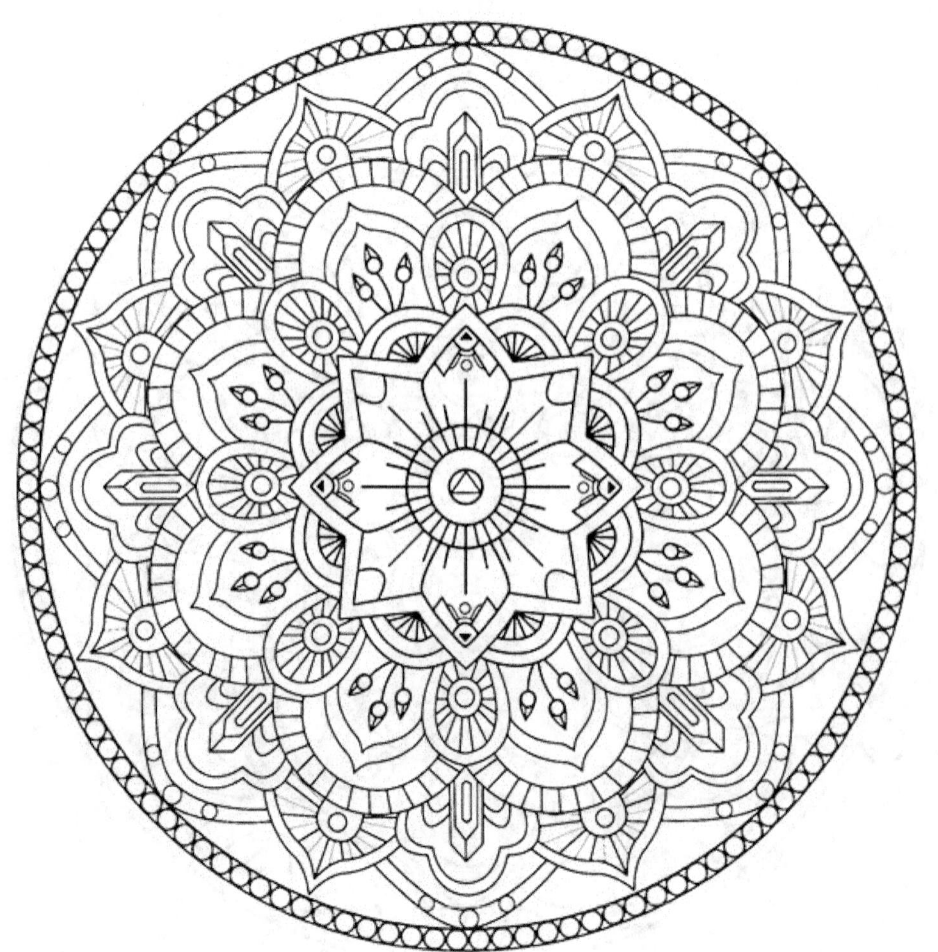

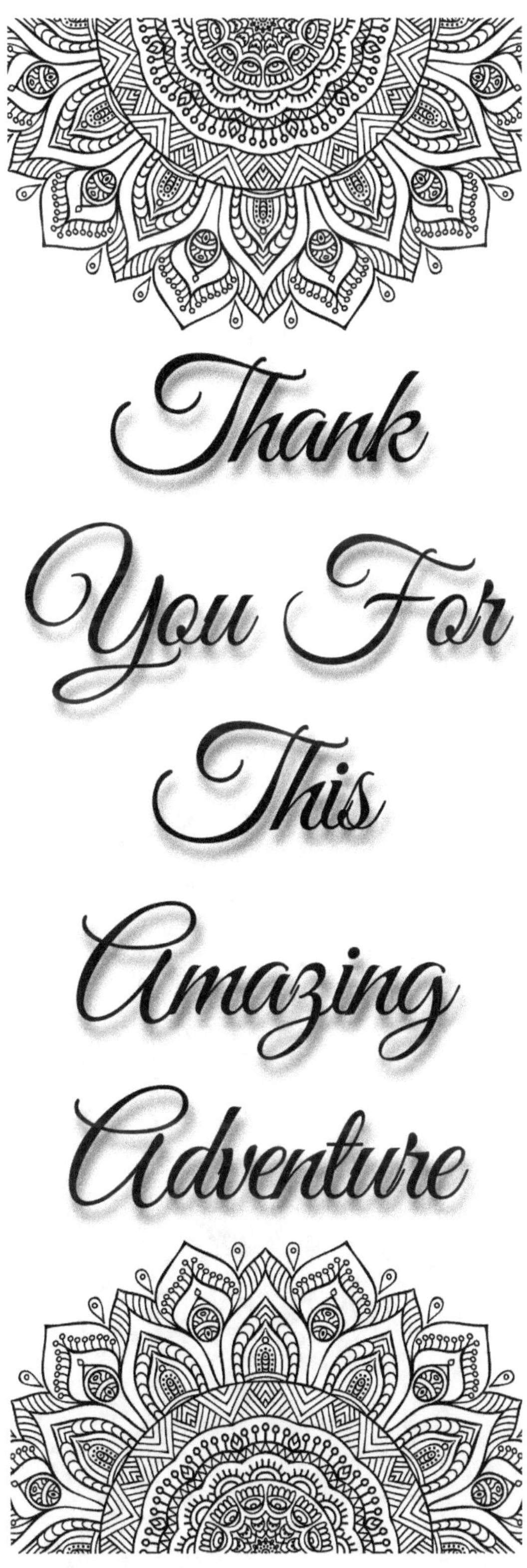

Thank
You For
This
Amazing
Adventure